Pundemonium
Vol. 4

James E. Larson

Lefse Press—Agoura Hills, Ca
ISBN: 979-8-9874392-6-5
eBook ISBN: 979-8-9874392-7-2
Title: *Pundemonium Vol. 4*
Author: James E. Larson
Digital distribution | 2023
Paperback | 2023

Dedication

The author dedicates this book to his loving family, wife Cindy, daughter Erica, and son Greg. They have had to listen to the author over the years trying out the various puns on them. They deserve recognition for enduring that pun-ishment.

Chapter One

An office worker was making adjustments to the very small pieces of film that his office keeps for their office records. He said to his coworkers, "Don't my improvements make the film more attractive and easier to work with?" All his coworkers said he was just fiching for compliments.

A man whose family is responsible to make sure the wire used in the high wire act at the local circus is safe was being interviewed. After he inspected the wire, he was asked by the reporter, "How do you people know the wire is ready?"

"Well," he said, "having the wire at the right tension is taut to us at a young age!"

Ted likes Christmas so much that during the Christmas Season, when he would order his favorite sandwich, which is a BLT (which stands for bacon, lettuce, and tomato), he would order it without lettuce. Even his sandwich had to have the Christmas spirit because it had no L in it.

The owner of a small sports car was having his car worked on at a small Junior College where students are taught how to repair the dents on a car's body. The cars accepted to be worked on have to have a large number of imperfections. The owner was so proud that his car made the Ding's List.

I heard the story about the guy who invented the clinging plastic wrap for food leftovers and how he was describing how he luckily came up with the product. He said it was saran-dipity....

A dining room table factory that makes extensions for your table tops hired an advertising company to come up with a new slogan to boost their sales. The slogan they came up with was "We Make Table Top Extensions So Leaf It to Us!"

A Gambling Anonymous meeting was being held at a private residence. Suddenly one participant got up and ran and jumped around the room in a playful gesture. The person running the meeting stood up and said forcefully, "I said there will be no gamboling in this house!"

Chapter Two

At a river's edge in the old west, two inept men were trying to tie logs together to make something that would float them down the river. Their incompetence at binding a bunch of logs together was the source of a raft of jokes by the nearby spectators.

The rebellious stockholders of a pancake liquid topping company took surprise control over the owner of the business. The local business newspaper said what the stockholders essentially did to the owner was usurp him.

A man was arrested in Czechoslovakia the other day because he was hiding some criminals in his house from the police. The police charged him for the caching of bad Czechs....

An old show business veteran, whose act was appearing in white face and not saying anything but acting out daily routines, had hired a young fellow to copy him in the act. After a few months, the veteran was worried that his partner wanted to leave and start his own act. The veteran thought he was beginning to lose his mime.

A cat burglar stole some jewelry and left no trace of him being there. It was the purr-fect crime.

A young man in the old west decided to make a boat out of some old sheet metal by heating up the metal and shaping it into a boat. He was not sure it was going to float but he forged ahead anyway.

I heard of a juggler that years ago had an act where he juggled small Dalmatian dogs. When he was juggling well, he was spot on.

In Germany, a man was on a computer site for a cloud storage system for photos that had somehow failed to allow any storage of photos. Then for some reason all of a sudden, he was in a state of perfect happiness. That's when he discovered he was on Cloud Nein!

Chapter Three

In a brand new house for sale, the computer people were hooking everything in the kitchen up to a laptop computer so everything would turn on with one stroke of keyboard. They hooked up the stove, refrigerator, all the lights, microwave oven. Then they left. They hooked up everything but the kitchen sync.

There is an Italian bakery in Boston that has a Halloween costume contest every year where the winner wins some pastry in the store. Last year's winner wore a Star Wars costume. The headline in the local paper the next day was "Obi Won Cannoli!"

A professional float builder was hired to produce a very large head with a window in the neck so the people inside the head could see out. Well, the builder had a lot of trouble getting that window just right. He said that getting that window installed was a pane in the neck!

When ten year old Billy found out that they would not have his favorite toothpaste at camp grounds this year, he was crestfallen.

The snake wrangler on the Cleopatra movie set filming in Egypt wanted to be the best snake wrangler in the business. He had high asp-irations....

At a local County Fair, the owner of a large male sheep was having a hard time controlling his animal. That animal was jumping around all over the place. A County Fair official asked the owner, "Is that animal always that ram-bunctious?"

There was an old county music singer in the back woods of Georgia that only sang songs about fireplace fires. He took the stage name of "Hearth Brooks."

At a Jewelry Show, a designer created earrings that each had a ten cent coin hanging from them. He hired some really beautiful models to wear the earrings around the show. The orders for the earrings came in quickly. The designer said his success was due to the paradigm's unique appeal.

Chapter Four

A thief broke into the local armory and he started to rifle through the inventory.

A local dude ranch relocated nearby to the Getty Center in Los Angeles in hopes of generating more business for the dude ranch. The owner named the ranch "Getty Up!"

An ornithologist was studying the mating habits of a certain bird that lives on the coastal beaches. He discovered that the well behaved birds of that species would attract and mate with other well behaved birds of that species. At the conclusion of his study, he proclaimed that "One good tern deserves another."

When Vincent van Gogh cut off part of his body, people around him thought that it seemed kind of eerie.

A writer that liked to write about jungle animals wrote an article praising the attributes of the large animal, the hippo. A few weeks later, he was paid a nice sum of money to write a disparaging article about the same animal. His fellow writers thought he was being a little hippo-critical.

In Nepal, the country of the mountain range where Mount Everest is located, a law enforcement officer was following a man who was a robbery suspect around a small village on a very cold day. The officer saw the suspect go into a house. The officer knocked on the front door and a lady came to see what the officer wanted. The officer asked the lady where was the man who just came into her house. She replied, "Come with me to the kitchen, Himalayan on the floor by the kitchen heater."

The guy who owned a candy factory that made the small thin green color wafers was asked why he decided to make that kind of candy. He said, "I guess it was just mint to be!"

Chapter Five

Noah, for whatever reason, did not like those dairy animals and was not going to take them on the ark. After talking with his boss, he did take those animals on the ark, but he always felt he was cowed into it....

In New York City, near the Lincoln Center, there is a footwear shop that caters to ballerinas. The store sells an earthy, woody foot spray perfume that is quite popular. They call the spray, "The Toe Musk Go On!"

A farmer in Illinois was in a government program where he was paid to not farm part of his farm's acreage. A government inspector caught him one day as the farmer was growing crops on that acreage. The farmer just didn't fallow the land guidelines.

A geologist was writing a book about the structures that are put across rivers to create lakes behind them. He quit writing the book halfway through as he got tired of the whole dam thing.

A secretary in New York City wanted to take a day off so she was talking to her boss on the phone and telling her why she couldn't come into work this day. The secretary just had her hair styled and she knew it looked terrible. However, she didn't want to lie to her boss so she said, "I really have a bad coif!"

Down at the marina, an auction was going to be held for the many old ocean going floating devices that warn sailors of dangers on the ocean. When the doors to the auction house opened, a stampede of men rushed to check out the condition of the devices and the mob disrupted everything. The chief of security was told to go into the mob and separate the men from the buoys.

The owner of a moving company, who always wanted to be in show business, wrote an original musical play about a magical four wheel low moving platform that thinks it's an angel. The name of the play is "Halo Dolly!"

Chapter Six

I heard about a former plumber who now works as a chef in a vegan restaurant. That restaurant only serves vegetables, especially those large ones in the onion family. He may have changed jobs, but it seems he continues to be working on leeks.

Bill owned a wooden barrel manufacturing company in Kentucky that sold barrels to companies that made whiskey. One day Bill heard some bad news. A competing barrel company had relocated nearby and they were making barrels at a cheaper price. So Bill was going to have to find a cheaper way to make the wooden parts of the barrel and try to stave off the competition.

In old Elizabethan England, in a small village next to a lake, two unpleasant, annoying women were on a ladder, with the bottom of the ladder in the lake, arguing over who should get to the top of the ladder first and then onto the dock. One fell off. The villagers who were in the water were left wadding for the other shrew to drop.

Just think about how hard it was for the son of the "Invisible Man" to go door to door selling candy for new band uniforms. All the homeowners said they could see right through him....

Only in Russia does their government name a person who becomes responsible for all the honey production and the honey production insects in the whole vast country. I don't know if you agree, but that is some Bee Czar appointment!

In a small county in Southeast Asia, there is a restaurant that charges customers a fee to soak their tea bags. Every time the restaurant raises their price for soaking the customers' tea bags, it is a steep increase.

The happy-go-lucky, indifferent owner of a Japanese restaurant that serves raw fish has an in-sushi-ant attitude.

Chapter Seven

In a hat store in New York City, one of the two owners started a new customer service. A customer could grab a hat off the shelf and replace the hat on the shelf with a small hand written piece of paper with the customer's name, address, and the amount of money the customer owes the store. The other owner found out about this service and did not like it. The two owners, after they argued about it, agreed to get rid of that concept and decided to bury the hat chit.

I heard an oceanographer located on the shores of Mexico has successfully taught a dolphin to sing. The oceanographer could not find any musicians to accompany the dolphin in the water so the dolphin had to sing aqua-pella.

A little known fact is that there is a small city in the state of Illinois that has a sister city in Alaska. That small city also has a radio station that has a show hosted by a lady named Alice who on the show goes on and on and on without saying much. However, she could poke fun at herself and at the same time publicize an event that occurs in that sister city in Alaska by the name she selected for her radio show. The name she picked was, "The Aurora Boring Alice Show."

In the deep South, two inept moonshiners were making their product in an old cabin. They got word two government agents were coming to their place in a few minutes.

One man said, "We have to hide our moonshine, but where?"

The other man pointed over to the front door that had a hollow core and was slightly open. He said that was a good thing the door was slightly open as they had access to the top of the door in which to pour their moonshine.

He added, "We could only see to use the door because it was ajar!"

Two retirees from China living in southern Florida, were fixing up their house boat. The wife was arranging the pieces in the living spaces to create a balance with the natural world. They were anticipating having a lot of Feng Shui down upon the Swanee River.

Chapter Eight

There was a bartender I know who knew an awful lot about many things that swim in the ocean, however, he always drank too much liquor at one time. He would drink like aficionado.

A former boxer was really out of shape. His stomach was so big and extended that whenever he bent over too quickly, he would always get a paunch in the face.

A large company that makes the butter substitute margarine as its product, was remodeling its lobby in the company headquarters. The company officers wanted the floor to be wood with a pattern that would reflect well on the company. So, it made sense the pattern they chose was parquet.

A young electrician, who was attending a trade school, was studying for an upcoming test on the history of bulbs. At night, he was looking forward to a little light reading before he went to sleep.

In a small rural town in Iowa, time passes so slowly there that sometimes they don't get their June Bugs till August. When a lot of them do appear, the town provides a lecture on main street called, "If A June Bug Eschewing Your Plant's Leaves Happens, Why That's A Good Thing!"

In a small village in Thailand, there is a little shop that makes a thick sweet liquid that you can pour on pancakes. The shop makes that liquid from the glands of non-toxic snakes found in that village. The name of that product is "Syrup-entine."

I don't know if this is believable, but I heard about a very small town in the Midwest that in order to keep their High School open, the school officials allowed certain woolly farm animals to be counted as part of their student body. The school did not have to teach them anything because those "students" already had their sheepskins. Some female members of that group, I was told, went onto the university called "What's The Matter Ewe."

Chapter Nine

A young rancher in Montana needed some cash in a hurry so he sold one of his very young horses. Right away he had some foal-ding money.

Do you all remember the children's T V show "The Banana Splits?" When they were in their banana car, they would always floor the accelerator, spin their tires and peal out down the road.

An old jazz musician, whose job was to drive a bus, would play his saxophone while he was driving. He would play with other musicians traveling on the bus even when it was time to pull over for a rest period. He was always known as the driver who likes to jam on the breaks no matter what.

The chef came into the kitchen and discovered a cat was running about and dragging things off the shelves. Just then, the assistant chef came into the kitchen and just happened to see the cat run out of the room dragging a kitchen utensil. The chef did not say anything, so the assistant asked the chef, "Cat got your tong?"

The president of the company that makes sharp cutting hand tools that chop down trees was evaluating their new young employee. The employee's job was to assemble the pieces of the cutting hand tool but he was having trouble. However, to his benefit, he kept trying to get his axe together.

In the old west, ranch owners who had cow hands that continuously spoke only in senseless talk and nonsense were always sent to the bunk house.

An old used tire salesman was selling his under inflated tires at a flat rate.

I heard an old story about an army sent out from ancient Rome that got lost in the desert for almost a year. They were lost but they never lost their identity or where they were from as they were still Roman in the desert all that time.

An ornithologist was studying the common relatively small bird with very dark black feathers. He discovered that the bird did the same ordinary things every day. He thought that was very crow-tidian.

Chapter Ten

A young businessman had a combination business where he would lease trash containers out to customers and also he would act as a bill collector for people. The sign on the wall outside his office said, "BIN THERE/DUN THAT!"

Did you know about this little known fact that Russia's first satellite was just a sack of potatoes? You never heard of "Spudnik?"

A man was buying a factory that produces inflatable items that you tie to the end of a string and that are enjoyed by kids at birthday parties. A detail at the end of the agreement to buy the factory was that the seller was to receive a balloon payment.

In Spain, a local candy maker thought about combining the fruit of a tree native to the Mediterranean area with a small green thin sweet wafer. Alas, it was only a fig-mint of his imagination.

Off the coast of Italy, an oceanographer was studying eels and their mating habits. He found the more gentle and loving eels were quicker to mate. He said, "I guess that is why they are called a Moray eel."

Believe it or not, I heard there was a small traveling Flea Circus years ago in a small European Country that had another act like the fleas. The circus had a man who had trained some ants to do acrobatics. Nobody knew if the man was serious or not about the presentation as the name he chose for the act was "Flip-Ant!"

Did you hear about the owl that had laryngitis? He couldn't give a hoot about it.

A person was doing research about why in the Old West the wagon following a cowboys' cattle drive was named a chuck wagon. One explanation was that the cut of the beef from a cow's neck is called chuck. I prefer the other story which is how the cowboys, after being served a bad tasting meal, would chuck their plates toward the wagon.

Chapter Eleven

In England, a couple of young masseuses were experimenting with different items to exfoliate the skin of customers. They found out that the rough crust of freshly baked bread worked very well. Soon after, they advertised their shop with the slogan, "Don't Be Late, Exfoliate with a Full Loofah Bread!"

In the old West, an old prospector brought in a small sack of minerals from his mine to a shop that analyzes the composition of the minerals. The shop owner gave the prospector a real long report on the minerals. I guess the shop owner had plenty to assay about the sample.

A long time ago, there was a mail delivery system where the horse riders would ride a long distance then switch horses and ride another long distance. The starting point for this system was St. Joesph, Missouri. On every anniversary on the day this mail delivery system started, a local coffee house offers a drink called the "Pony Espresso!"

There is a story going around that even Cupid sometimes has supply problems. When he tries to get people together, he unfortunately every now and then runs out of eros.

A medical factory that makes the thin translucent fabric with an open weave that people use on open wounds on the body has come up with a new sales slogan. The slogan is, "Please Use Our Product, Gauze It Works Really Well!"

An eccentric cobbler, who ran a small shoe store, thought each pair of shoes had their own personality. He said he could tell when they were happy or sick. In fact, he thought he was the only one that could make the sick pairs feel better when he would install the last part at the rear of the shoe and heal them.

At a cherry processing factory company picnic, one of the events is to have cherry fights with teams throwing cherries at each other that still have their seeds inside. The owner of the factory enjoys pitting one team against the other.

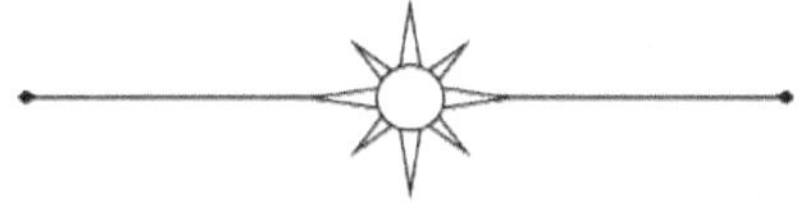

Chapter Twelve

Are people who say the Easter Bunny does not exist committing hare-esy?

A promoter, in a way to make some quick money, planned to put on an event where at a race track, he would race a horse against a deer. The promoter just happened to have a deer he had rescued in a forest. He said he planned to train the deer to run as fast as it could. So in the end, the promoter was just trying to make a fast buck.

There was a critic that wrote reviews for movies. Some movie producers did not like his reviews and told him so. The reviewer held his ground and kept showing the public at large how writing reviews was a special skill for him. He said sometimes you just have to keep sticking your knack out.

A young, sometimes confused, student oceanographer decided he would study the social habits of shrimp. He did observe that they did not seem to share their food with each other. He said he was not surprised as he already heard the shrimp were shell fish.

Down on a small chicken farm, a farmer's daughter was at first afraid to remove the feathers from a chicken. But after a while, she was the best child the farmer had to do this task. You could say she became one plucky kid!

A landscape contractor installed an orchard of one type of fruit tree that produces a purple fleshy fruit with a hard fruit seed inside. The contractor was so happy to do the work. He considered it was a plum job for him.

A refuse collection company was trying to give their best long time employee a raise. The employee kept saying the offers were too low and he called their offers trash. Finally, the company gave the employee what he wanted. They made him an offer that he couldn't refuse.

In a Southeastern Asian country, a bread baker would sell with every loaf a small Buddha figurine. This was the baker's bread and Buddha.

Chapter Thirteen

Somehow on a famous island mentioned in the movie South Pacific, a man built a roller coaster. For the children who want to ride it, there is a height requirement and they must be Bali Hai....

The drivers of two freeway service trucks that remove broken down cars off the freeways decided to have a contest. The contest was who could get more cars off the freeways in 24 hours. The drivers, who really didn't like each other, were going tow to tow.

The teenager was before the judge. The teenager was caught covering a stature at City Hall with aluminum wrap, the kind a person would have in their kitchen. The judge asked the teenager why he did that to the stature. The teenager said, "I was just foiling around!"

An old eccentric lumberjack in the backwoods was going bald. So he had an idea he would make head coverings out of finely, tiny, thin branches woven together. He thought he could maybe sell them as he had come up with a catchy name for them.

"No," said his friend after he saw one example, "nobody is going to buy your 'TWigs.'"

In London a long time ago, there was a man known for stopping by some old widower's house and asking them if they would like to have a new front entry step installed. He would take their money in advance and then build a front step that was so poorly made and was always a few inches lower than it should be and then he would leave town. The police detective assigned to the case was overheard saying, "I don't know how a man could stoop that low!"

I heard a garden supply store in the old south now offers the following service. If you have a garden fence supported by long wooden poles in the ground that have broken off at the base, the store will conduct a postmortem on the fence post and tell you why it broke off.

The old antique clock dealer had passed away and his widow decided to sell his business. Getting ready for the auction, she spent the rest of the time in his shop winding up his estate.

Chapter Fourteen

An almost two year old boy named Wyatt, who was talking more all the time, had a mother who was showing him two picture books almost every day. One was about "Robbin Hood and his Merry Men" and the other was all about fire trucks. When asked what was his most favorite thing in each of the two books, he thought for a moment, smiled, and said, "Friar Tuck!"

I heard that a very paranoid carpenter quit working on the construction of some steps because he thought they were staring at him.

I heard a retired dentist, who just loves Venice, Italy, has a multi-family housing development he started years ago in Arizona next to the old Highway Route 66. The dentist designed the development so that the only way to get around within the area from point to point would be by the water way canals within the project. Some locals who were not fond of the dentist called those water ways his "Route Canals."

The editor of a horse racing magazine wanted to generate some new interest in his magazine. He thought he would hire an analytics and advisory company to survey hundreds of thoroughbred race horse owners and ask them what is it about the horse that allows it to run so fast. The editor told his assistant to hire the appropriate best firm for the job so the assistant thought about it and went out and hired The Gallop Poll.

A large company, that makes chemicals that dissolve other chemicals, put out a press release the other day. They announced they have come back from the edge of financial trouble and they will also not expand into other products. The company will remain solvent.

In a recent bulletin, the travel agents that will book travelers into Hawaii airports during this upcoming winter holiday season, announced that the procedure for refusing the flowered necklaces you typically receive upon your arrival in Hawaii has been streamlined. You can notify your travel agent ahead of time using their concept which is called, "The Lei-Away Plan."

Chapter Fifteen

In a well-known restaurant, there is a cook whose responsibility is ordering, from the food suppliers, only the short extruded angular cut type of pasta. He keeps bargaining with the suppliers to give him the lowest price possible. The suppliers call him the "Penne Pincher!"

An old guy just came to the city and got a job with a shop that makes thin wide flat pieces of wood that you attach to walls so you can put items on the flat pieces of wood. He said he always wanted to be shelf-employed.

A farmer in Iowa was using a tractor to drag a large farm implement across a field that was leveling the soil in his fields. All of a sudden his tractor caught on fire. "Oh No!" he thought, "I am just going from one harrowing experience to another!"

The owners of a hot dog factory were talking about how to improve their product. They were having a frank discussion.

A carpenter just recently took a very comprehensive test where he had to identify all the many different types of wood planks. He now considered himself to be board certified.

A computer wizard helped a musical band of young dentists write an app that would help them book live performances. The app is called "Gigabyte."

A very large sumo wrestler, who acted silly, pointless, and foolish most of the time, was trying to find a stage name for his future matches. A critic for a wrestling magazine came up with a name that seemed to stick. The name he came up with was "Fatuous!"

A party planner was known to throw some bad parties. In fact, not many people wanted to go to them. Most of them said going to any party she puts on would be a fete worse than death.

Chapter Sixteen

id you hear about the story that the inventor of "Teflon" was getting sued all the time by his competitors who thought he did things illegally to achieve his fame. His competitors told the authorities to charge him with a crime but the authorities could never get anything to stick.

During basic training for a fireman recruit, the recruit got a fear of going above the second floor of a building. However, he finally got over it and that's another story.

The professional softball pitcher's honesty was being questioned in a court deposition because during her career she was always doing things underhanded.

An old person in a small village in Bavaria made a musical instrument from a couple of dried pumpkins that you could squeeze together and pull apart to make musical notes. He calls his instrument the Agourdian.

In Germany, when the food experts tell you what kind of meat is bad for you, they will often tell you that in addition to the over salted sausage tasting bad, it is also named as the wurst.

A housewife was shopping for a table lamp. She narrowed it down to two lamps that were side by side at the store. It came down to her choice of the decorative fabric item atop the lamp which diffuses the light of the light bulb. The one she chose is the one she liked a shade better.

An ornithologist was observing a small brown song bird with a tail that points upward. He noticed that when the bird came upon an old abandoned nest, the bird started to rearrange things. The ornithologist said to himself, "That bird is obviously making Wrenovations!"

The City ordered a homeowner to install a railing along a sidewalk on his property. The homeowner disagreed and went to City Hall to argue against the order. The homeowner spent his time railing against the railing.

Chapter Seventeen

A company that makes the soft cloth that goes atop pool tables announced that they would replace the old worn existing pool table cloth on the single pool table in the local YMCA without charge. The company president said, "I felt it was the right thing to do!"

At the local karaoke bar, it was "Bring Your Pet to Sing with You!" night. A man comes in with a snake and when it was his turn, he goes on stage. When the karaoke machine started playing "Welcome to the Jungle," the snake started to shake, hit a high note and made musical hissssstory!

A local politician, whose hobby was being a spelunker, was one day thinking about his desire to run for national office. However, when he thought he might have to give up his hobby because he would be so busy being a national politician, he realized then his only option about his desire was to cave.

A small perfume company, that was in financial trouble, was trying to come up with a new fragrance by combining two different smells. However, the company went broke before that could happen. The company showed that it could not even rub two scents together.

This is just a rumor, but I heard with all this gender talk, Hershey's candy bar company might come out with a Himshey candy bar....

There is a funny doctor I know that after an operation keeps you in stitches while he sews you up.

The company that made projectors that shines a light through a transparent photograph in a carousel onto a silver screen has gone out of business due to lack of demand. The company did not try to get into new technology to save the company. They just kept letting everything slide.

Chapter Eighteen

In ancient Greece, there was a play about a man who goes to a tailor shop which is run by the owner of the shop. The dialogue in the opening scene goes like this when the patron goes into the shop with his damaged toga, "Euripides?" asks the shop owner.

"Eumendides?" asks the patron.

Two trapeze artists were trying out some new tricks for their act but they were unsure if they would incorporate them into their show. Their decision about adding the new tricks was still up in the air.

A pair of Russian marathon runners in a race in Western Russia were planning to defect to the country located between Sweden and Russia. Suddenly they left the official race course and ran toward the border. They were so happy when they finally crossed the Finish line.

The delicatessen owner was trying new toppings for his bagels. A customer asked why is he doing that. The owner said, "Sometimes you have to think outside the lox."

Some people use the large antlers from a deer, after the antlers fall off, as the basis of a chandelier light headed for their cabins. It is only fitting as I am sure after the antlers fall off the deer, the deer feels light headed also.

A high school chemistry teacher divided his class into four groups each with a name of a major element as the groups' name like "The Lead Group." Questions would be asked in rapid fire time of each group by another group about the characteristics of their element name. If the group failed to answer fast enough they were eliminated. Student Leo would lead "The Lead Group" but he could not lead them to victory as they were the first to be eliminated. The game proceeded quickly after that as the other groups got the Lead out.

Chapter Nineteen

The owner of a factory that makes wooden window coverings, that have slats in them, was worried about the new trend of building houses without window coverings. He said, "I shutter to think about that!"

COOKING 101: Always look at everything that is cooking so that there are no surprises especially if you get side tracked focusing on taking the skin off of potatoes. Especially when you are doing potatoes you should keep your eyes peeled.

I heard a story about an explorer, named Jeff, who was in a jungle but he was feeling very sick and was very pale. All of a sudden, he comes face to face with another explorer. Jeff came to the conclusion that the other explorer was in the same medical condition as himself. After I heard this story, I realized it is true that it takes wan to know wan!

A civil engineer that has constructed miles and miles of highways decided he would go to the University of Oxford in Oxford, England to further his education. He also got a scholarship to attend. He thought it would be fitting to be a civil engineer and be known as a "Rhodes Scholar."

The father was giving his daughter away at the wedding at their house. His daughter was his bride and joy!

I know a pundamentalist who was getting married. He liked to put puns on everything and so he attached one to his belt/sash that goes around his waist and comes with the tuxedo. He called it his cumberpun.

The Procrastinaters Club members were going to have a joint meeting with members of the Apathy Club but the meeting got postponed to next week. Half of the expected attendees thought that was a good idea while the other half didn't seem to care.

I heard about a man from Poland who was always upbeat and because of that, he drew lots of people around him, People would say he was a positive Pole with a resulting magnetic personality.

In the Queens Court in London, they appointed a new person to write new poems and read them for all Court members. The person appointed happened to be a long time cowboy who knew many rope tricks. The London press has nicknamed the new member as the "Poet Lariat."

In Germany at a Police Station, they had an undercover operation going on where they were trying to get a gang member to report back to the police about the gang's activities. The Chief of Police said the only way it would save him from saying no to disbanding this operation is if the informant would start reporting. Finally the gang member started talking. This was another case where "A Snitch in Time saves Nien!"

About the Author

The author, James E. Larson, has always enjoyed a good pun. Just recently, he decided to create new ones for a book. He says like anything else, some puns come easy while other need some rewrites before they are finished. A good pun needs a good back story that sets up the 'Pun-ch Line.' That is the fun part of creating puns.